ABRAHAM LINCOLN

The American Civil War
and the Abolition of Slavery

Written by Mélanie Mettra
In collaboration with Christelle Klein-Scholz
Translated by Rose Brichard

History 50MINUTES.com

ABRAHAM LINCOLN

KEY INFORMATION

- **Born:** 12 February in Harding County (Kentucky)
- **Died:** 14 April in Washington
- **Political party:** The Republican Party
- **Dates elected:**
  - 6 November 1860
  - 8 November 1864
- **Time in office:** 4 years
- **Major achievements:**
  - The Abolition of Slavery
  - The *Homestead Act*
  - Upholding National Unity
  - Building the Pacific Railroad

INTRODUCTION

Abraham Lincoln, known as "The Great Emancipator" and whose face is carved into Mount Rushmore, is without a doubt one of the most celebrated figures of American history. Though he had a modest upbringing and was largely self-taught, he managed to climb his way to the top of the political ladder and become the 16th President of the United States through his tireless work ethic and unrelenting will. Despite the fact that his election triggered the American Civil War, in just one presidential term he managed to restore national unity and resolve the questions surrounding slavery which had troubled the country since its inception. While the huge scale of the Civil War tends to obscure

Lincoln's other achievements as President, they are nonetheless many; it was under Lincoln that Americans would see their country reconstructed largely thanks to Lincoln's wartime economy, the regulation of property rights and the construction of the railway system.

BIOGRAPHY

Portrait of Abraham Lincoln, dated 1863.

YOUTH

Abraham Lincoln was born on 12 February 1809 in Hardin County, Kentucky. A child of the frontier, Lincoln grew up in a very modest family. His father Thomas Lincoln (1778-1851) was an illiterate American farmer who left Kentucky to settle in Indiana when his son was just seven years old.

Soon after, the young Abraham Lincoln's mother died; he found his stepmother Sarah Bush Lincoln (1788-1869) to be an unwavering support. As a farm boy, he received no regular schooling and tried his hand at various different lines of work. He worked as a boatman, hired to move goods down the Mississippi river, and made his own barge to transport raw materials all the way to New Orleans. When he settled in New Salem, Illinois in 1831, he went from being a postman to a surveyor to a store clerk. He earned a reputation for himself as a jovial and lively character and was renowned for his services as a scribe for the poorest members of society.

GOOD TO KNOW

As one of the foundations of the American collective imagination, the frontier represents the line between colonised territories and the vast expanse of wild untamed land which lay beyond, existing somewhere between civilization and savagery. It embodies more than a physical border; it was the promise of a new world to conquer, an image of hope as much as fear. The physical frontier was pushed further and further back during the 19th century as the West was colonised. In 1890 the frontier lapsed into non-existence when all the land had finally been claimed. From then on, the frontier no longer signified anything official even though certain areas remained unexplored. This marked the end of an era in which the American territory was conceived of in this light. The frontier took on a mythical quality from then on and is still an endless source of inspiration for literature and cinema.

LINCOLN'S DEBUT ON THE POLITICAL SCENE

In 1832, Lincoln signed up as a volunteer in the local militia to help fight in a territorial conflict against Native Americans led by Black Hawk (Native American Chief, 1767-1838). He then made his debut on the political scene by standing as a candidate in the Illinois state House of Representatives election. He was not elected despite the huge majority he received in New Salem. Lincoln did not give up on his political dream however, and began studying law to help him in this quest. He graduated law school and received his law degree in 1837 before moving to Springfield.

In 1834, he stood once again as a candidate for the Illinois House of Representatives and this time he was successful. In this new position, he developed himself politically and made his abolitionist views heard. He then won the seat as Congressman for Illinois as a Whig, keeping his views on tensions with Mexico quiet during his campaign. Once elected, he was quick to denounce President James Knox Polk's (1795-1849) administration for its hypocrisy with regards to the Mexican-American War (1846-1848). He refuted the claims that in entering into war with Mexico the United States was merely retaliating against Mexican attacks. He instead argued that the attacks had been entirely reciprocal and based upon disputed ownership of territories around the border between the two countries. This overt opposition cost him his seat in Congress, and he temporarily withdrew from the world of politics, giving up on the likely possibility of becoming Illinois state senator.

THE ELECTION WHICH TRIGGERED A CIVIL WAR

From 1856 onwards, Lincoln established ties with the new Republican Party, formed by former members of the Whig Party, the Democratic Party and the Free Soil Party, who were all strongly opposed to slavery. Lincoln ran for Vice-President of the party but was unsuccessful. When he was chosen by his peers as a candidate for the Senate in 1858, he led a tough campaign against his opponent Stephen Arnold Douglas (1813-1861) of the Democratic Party. Despite his brilliant repartees in the verbal duels which took place between the two, Lincoln lost the election. He nonetheless earned himself a certain notoriety after the campaign. Two years later in November 1860, made a bid for the American presidency. The Democratic Party divided, Lincoln received almost 40% of the vote despite the three candidates running against him; this was enough to secure his victory. When this openly anti-slavery candidate was announced as the new President of the United States, South Carolina seceded and was followed by several other Southern states who together founded a new confederation in February 1861. The Civil War began when these new Confederationists attacked Fort Sumter in April 1861. Though Lincoln was originally the commander of the Northern army, he transferred this responsibility to Ulysses Simpson Grant (future U.S. President, 1822-1885) so he could dedicate himself to the political matters at hand.

The bombing of Fort Sumter.

A NEW ERA

To finance the Civil War, Lincoln was quick to impose a tax on revenues. His secretary of the Treasury Salmon Portland Chase (1808-1873) introduced the first paper currency (called greenbacks), not backed by gold or silver. On 20 May 1862, the Homestead Act (property law) was ratified. This act regulated access to private property rights and launched the first railroad constructions in the country. On 2 January 1863, the Emancipation Proclamation came into force: all slaves in the rebel states were declared free. This provoked outrage among anti-abolitionists and assassination plots against the President were devised. Lincoln remained undeterred and tried to entrench the abolition of slavery in the United States Constitution by submitting the proposition to the Senate in April 1864 and then to

Congress in January 1865. Though this decision was indeed adopted after much virulent and animated debate, Lincoln, re-elected in November 1864, would not live to see it finally ratified by the majority of the states nor coming into action in December 1865. Just a few months before this on 14 April 1865, Lincoln was shot as he attended a play with his wife by John Wilkes Booth (1838-1865), a young Confederate sympathiser. He died the following morning and his body was taken to Illinois to be buried.

The assassination of President Lincoln.

a monument in his honour in Oak Ridge Cemetery in Springfield. This called for several provisional tombs during the process. However, his corpse was exhumed again several years after his assassination in 1876, when "Big Jim" Kinealy tried to steal it to use as a bargaining tool in an attempt free his partner who was in prison for forgery. Kinealy and his accomplices only managed to uproot the tombstone before they were caught by the authorities. From then on, Lincoln's son Robert Todd Lincoln (1943-1926) ordered that the tomb be secured in order to keep it safe. This in turn gave rise to further exhumations of the body.

POLITICAL, SOCIAL AND ECONOMIC CONTEXT

THE CHANGING FACE OF POLITICS

The first half-century of the United States' existence is marked by the birth, development and maturation of different strands of political thought which were subsequently expressed in party-political terms. These parties formed, split up and dissolved as political standpoints polarised and became clearer. Under the Washington (1732-1799), Adams (1735-1826) and Jefferson (1743-1826) administrations, two schools of thought divided the political playing field into two distinct camps: the Federalists and the Democratic-Republicans. The principle differences in their views concerned their conceptions of the roles and powers of the federal government. As the years went on, these two political families evolved. The Federalist Party, in favour of a closer relationship with Great Britain, did not survive the war of 1812-1814. The Democratic-Republican Party splintered off in 1828 following the election of Andrew Jackson (1767-1845) and in light of the slavery question which divided its membership. While some of its members followed John Quincy Adams (1767-1848, president from 1825 to 1829) in opposing slavery, others sided with Andrew Jackson and created the Democratic Party, supported by the pro-slavery camp and notably represented by John Caldwell Calhoun (American politician, 1782-1850).

The Whig Party appeared several years later in response to the policies of President Andrew Jackson, re-elected for a second term in 1832. It brought together industrialists, farmers and planters and championed the supremacy of Congress over the president, whom they considered to be autocratic in his rule. The party developed its doctrine following on from the successes of its four presidential candidates, and favoured a modernised economy based on commerce and exchange, and dynamic educational and cultural policy. They received widespread support from several big names in the newspaper world and counted Henry Clay (American politician, 1777-1852) and Abraham Lincoln among their members. From the 1850s onward however, the issue of slavery became more and more important and finally tensions born of this debate exploded and caused a deep rift within the Whig Party. The abolitionist members, including Lincoln, collaborated with the Free Soil Party - a party which disappeared almost as quickly as it came into existence - in a new political entity: the Republican Party. The Free Soil Party was formed for the 1848 presidential elections with a manifesto opposing the introduction of slavery to new territories and advocating free trade, enterprise and expression.

The newborn Republican Party adopted a resolutely anti-slavery programme in June 1856 which underlined Congress's incapacity to authorise slavery in any new state and its obligation to abolish slavery where it still existed. Their first presidential candidate, John Charles Fremont (1813-1890) was beaten by the Democrat James Buchanan (1791-1868) during the 1856 presidential elections. The Republicans won their first presidential victory four years later when Lincoln came to power.

A DEEPLY DIVIDED ECONOMY

Since the birth of the United States, the American economy had been divided into two major regions: the North, where the economy was based on industry and finance, and the South, where it was based on agriculture and trade. The North underwent a rapid industrialisation process thanks to two key factors. Firstly, foreign investment, which supported new mining technologies and facilitated the development of the metallurgical industry, which was in turn boosted by a revolution in transportation technology. Secondly, European investment. This foreign investment was however somewhat unreliable - subject to the unstable relations between America and its European partners and whether or not they proved to be reliable creditors. Therefore, the U.S. capitalist economy was regularly weakened by financial crises during the first half of the 19th century. It nonetheless continued to grow, largely supported by the gold rush which increased the overall money supply. In addition to this, European immigrants provided the workforce needed for the country to industrialise. They left Europe seeking their fortunes across the Atlantic from 1820 onwards, attracted by the newly industrialised textile industry, the growth of north-eastern cities and ports and the agricultural colonisation of central states. At first, most migration flows came from Northern Europe, followed by a huge wave of Irish migrants fleeing the great famine of 1845-1848. This foreign influx was a crucial factor in the country's economic development both with regards to industry and agriculture, though it also gave rise to new anti-immigrant sentiments embodied by the Know-Nothing movement.

The Know-Nothing movement arose in 19th century America in response to a wave of European migrants. In the 1850s, it grew to a level of major political importance and even established a political party. It represented American Nativist views and had its roots in secret orders such as the Order of the Star-Spangled Banner, invigorated by the presence of Irish Catholic migrants. Many American Protestants saw immigrants as a threat to both to the economy in that they were a source a cheap labour, and to American democracy, since one the foundations of Protestantism is a rejection of papal authority. The Know-Nothing movement disappeared as quickly as it took off, with all of the party members defecting to the newly-established Republican Party within just a few years.

While the northern states generally favoured trade protectionism in order to block imports of manufactured goods against which represented competition to their home-grown industries, the southern economy was based on exports and free trade. In fact, 70% of cotton produced in the South was destined for export, since its producers did not possess the tools necessary to manufacture textiles from their cotton. Furthermore, the southern economic structure, based on slave labour and dominated by several major planters, was favourable neither to immigration nor the development of free enterprise. As such, southern society was almost entirely dominated by what was in effect a conservative landed aristocracy. This deep north-south divide continued to breed tensions amid increasingly difficult relations within the federal government.

SLAVERY: THE ISSUE WHICH SPARKED SECESSION

The issue of slavery had been tormenting and dividing the United States ever since its birth as a new nation. It was already the subject of heated debate when the Constitution was drafted, raising questions which were never satisfactorily resolved. It was not until 1808 that the Constitution was adapted to forbid the importation of slaves. In any case, Article 4 stipulates that "No Person held to Service or Labour in one State, under the Laws thereof, escaping into another, shall, in Consequence of any Law or Regulation therein, be discharged from such Service or Labour, but shall be delivered up on Claim of the Party to whom such Service or Labour may be due". As such, the Constitution recognised the legitimacy of slave states and avoided any outright abolitionist legislation. Such a non-committal position was also the result of the Three Fifths Compromise which at once refused slaves the right to vote whether or not they had been freed, and counted three fifths of their overall number in a state's population, a figure which was used to determine the number of seats a state was entitled to in Congress. As such, the slave states were strongly represented and hoped to use this to strongly weigh in on the country's decision-making processes.

The U.S. Constitution therefore harboured conflicting

opinions right from the outset which were only aggravated by the Northwest Ordinance, announced in the same year as the Constitution. This act of Congress created a new Northwest Territory and set conditions of admission for candidate states which included a no-slavery requirement. Thus, a profound geographic cleavage with regards to slavery emerged between the North and South.

The situation remained largely stable until 1820 when Missouri - a slave-owning territory - requested access. It entered into the Federation and became the 24th state. However, this led to an increase in the number of pro-slavery members of the senate, which prompted anti-slavery activists to demand that slavery be abolished in Missouri. The Southern representatives rose up against this attempt by the Federal Government to intervene in state affairs. Senator Henry Clay tried to compensate for the strong pro-slavery political voice by proposing that Maine - an area in which slavery did not exist - be accepted as the 25th state. He then moved to establish a geographical boundary of 36º30' - in effect the edge of Missouri - beyond which slavery was prohibited. This was known as the Missouri Compromise and was accepted by both houses of Congress. Until the 1850s, every slave state which entered the federation was offset by the entry of a new free state to maintain a balance.

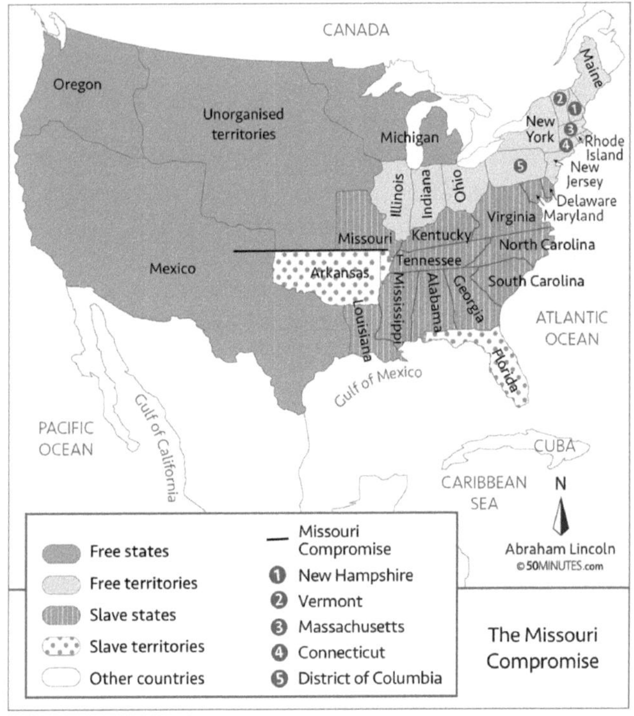

In 1850, a new compromise was necessary since the balance of pro and anti-slavery states was threatened by new states which entered as a result of the Mexican-American War. Clay, who was nicknamed The Great Compromiser, proposed a new text which legislated for:

- the admission of California as a free state
- New Mexico and Utah to have the right to decide whether to be free states or slave states

- a ban on the slave trade in the Columbia district
- a reaffirmation of the Fugitive Slave Act with regards to Article 4 of the Constitution, which required each state to return runaway slaves to their owner.

These apparent compromises did little to appease tensions. Instead, they polarised the political spectrum with regards to slavery even further. In the north, the idea of being part of a system they had publicly denounced decades before was a source of growing discontent, while in the south, the requirement that new states be free presented such a problem that some states were on the brink of secession.

The Kansas-Nebraska Act of 1854 created two new states which were free to choose whether or not to prohibit slavery within their boundaries. This repealed the precedent established in the Missouri Compromise since both Kansas and Nebraska were situated beyond the established geographical boundary and should therefore by law have been free states. This new law, championed by Senator Stephen Arnold Douglas of the Democrats, provoked outrage among the northern states. Both pro-slavery and abolitionist activists wreaked havoc in Kansas in an attempt to sway its decision.

Good to know

Between 1854 and 1861, many pro- or anti-slavery movements came into violent conflict with one another, particularly in Kansas. The Fire-Eaters were pro-slavery extremists who fought for the secession of the southern states in the 1850s. Their effective use of propaganda contributed to the country splitting in two when Lincoln was elected.

The Border Ruffians, a militia of landowners from Missouri which regularly led punitive expeditions to Kansas in the hope of imposing slave labour policies there, were another violent pro-slavery group. Driven out by the Kansas state governor, they continued their acts of violence and were quick to ally themselves with William Quantrill (1837-1865) and his band during the Civil War. This confederate guerilla leader, who had a particular appetite for terrorism and destruction through military discipline, marched through Kansas and carried out a raid on Lawrence in August 1863, in which he and his men massacred nearly 145 people and destroyed more than 100 buildings.

On the other side of the struggle was John Brown (1800-1859) whose activism turned to violence after one of his friends - a journalist - was killed. In 1855 he stabbed and killed multiple slave owners in Kansas and fought in the Battle of Osawatomie against the Border Ruffians in August 1856. He led a slave rebellion which began in 1857, but failed just two years later. When he attempted a raid on Harpers Ferry to carry out an armed slave revolt, he was captured by a platoon of U.S. marines led by Colonel Robert Edward Lee (future civil war general, 1807-1870). He was arrested and hanged, quickly becoming a martyr of the abolitionist cause.

The resolution of the Dred Scott case in 1857 in the Supreme Court further infuriated the northern states. Dred Scott was a former slave who had lived for several years with his master in the north before returning to Missouri on his master's death to enter into the service of his widow. He attempted to purchase he and his family's freedom, and when this was refused he resorted to legal action. He argued that since he had been a legal resident of a free state he had the right to emancipation. The Supreme Court, dominated by pro-slavery Justices, denied his request based on three main points:

- Since Dred Scott was of "the negro African race" he could not be considered as a citizen and thus did not have the right to sue.
- His stay in the free states did not give him the right to emancipation.
- The Missouri Compromise was unconstitutional; Congress did not have the right to decide whether or not a State should prohibit slavery since it infringed upon state competencies.

Deeply shocked by this decision, the abolitionists readied themselves for a political battle. Lincoln, a member of the newly-founded Republican Party, stood for election to the Senate in 1858 against Stephen Arnold Douglas. During the campaign, the two candidates took part in seven public debates which resulted in Lincoln losing the election. However, during his campaign, Lincoln gave speeches which would never be forgotten, such as *The House Divided Speech* which he delivered upon being nominated as his party's candidate in 1854, and the *Cooper Union Address*. These focussed on slavery and the very essence of the federal state system. From then on, his opponents regarded him as the terrifying political incarnation of abolitionism, and his presidential victory in 1860 almost immediately triggered the South's secession.

HIGHLIGHTS

Following his defeat in the Senate elections in 1858, Lincoln received the Republican nomination for the presidential elections of 1860 in the third round of voting.

The Democratic Party was deeply divided; if its pro-slavery members strongly asserted their views, the Democratic presidential candidate was sure to lose northern votes due to this radical standpoint. Therefore, even after 57 rounds of voting at the Charleston Convention in May 1860, no candidate could be chosen from the six competitors. One month later, the party splintered off into two camps, where the Northern delegates chose Stephen Arnold Douglas and the Southern delegates nominated John Cabell Breckinridge (1821-1875).

A fourth presidential candidate, John Bell (1796-1869), received the Unionist Party nomination. This party brought together members of the former Whig Party who had not joined the Republican Party.

During the campaign, political shots were fired from all directions. However, the Republican Party avoided the subject of slavery for fear of seeing southern states secede. Nonetheless, the results were clear evidence of a country divided into two clear zones. In November 1860, Lincoln received 54% of northern votes compared to just 4% in the South. On 20 December, the threat of secession materialised: South Carolina was the first to break away from the union, followed by Alabama, Mississippi, Georgia, Louisiana, Florida and Texas.

THE CIVIL WAR

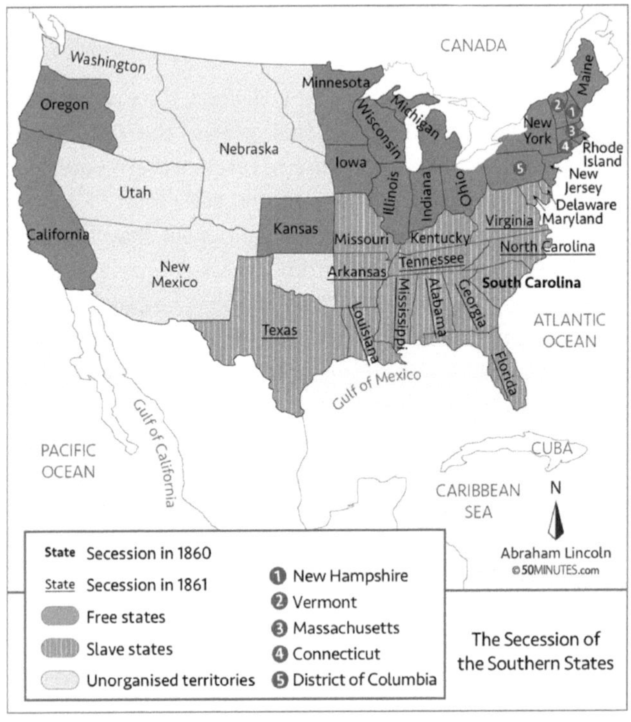

On 4 February 1861, the seceded states formed their own union called the Confederate States of America, with Jefferson Davis (1808-1889) as its temporary leader and

Richmond, Virginia as its capital city. The outgoing federal President James Buchanan denounced the secession as illegal and tried to resolve the issue diplomatically by proposing various compromises, all of which were refused by the Confederation. When Lincoln came to power, he was more prepared to envisage war as a means to solve the problem. This prospect soon became inevitable in the spring of 1861 when Confederate troops attacked the union garrison at Fort Sumter, South Carolina on 12 April. This attack occurred just a few weeks after Lincoln's inauguration as President and was led by General Pierre Gustave Toutant Beauregard (1818-1893). Lincoln was quick to mobilise 75 000 men and declare the Union Blockade. Subsequently, North Carolina, Arkansas, Tennessee and Virginia defected to the Confederation. From then on, the Civil War continued on two fronts: East and West, with the battlefields situated almost without exception on Confederate territory.

The beginning of the war was marked by Confederate victories in the East. General Beauregard's troops won the First Battle of Bull Run on 21 July 1861 while General Robert Edward Lee achieved victory over the Union army on Fredericksburg and Chancellorsville in December 1862 and May 1863 respectively. However, the Union army was more successful in the West, where General Ulysses Simpson Grant led his troops to victory in the Battle of Shiloh (6-7 April 1862). The Union naval forces, under the direction of General David Glasgow Farragut (1801-1870), successfully blocked the southern coasts and captured New Orleans in May 1862. Thereafter, the Union took definitive control of the Mississippi after the Siege of Vicksburg in July 1863, when they captured the last Confederate stronghold on the river. Fresh from his victory in Chancellorsville, General Robert Edward Lee attempted to invade the North but was defeated by General George Gordon Meade (1815-1872) and his troops in the Battle of Gettysburg on 3 July 1863. This is considered the bloodiest battle of the entire Civil War. Lincoln declared the Gettysburg battlefield as a national cemetery in November 1863 to honour the victims of both sides. It was here that Lincoln gave his famous *Gettysburg Address*, speaking of the American nation as the founding fathers imagined it, calling for the preservation of government for, by, and of the people.

This defeat was the Confederate army's swansong, its final performance before the Unionists. Led by General William Tecumseh Sherman (1820-1891), the Confederates marched through Georgia and the Carolinas, splitting the Confederation into two camps separated by a 50-kilometre strip of land devastated by war. Not long before Lincoln's re-election on 3 September 1864, they captured Atlanta. Richmond, the Confederate capital, fell on 3 April 1865. Three days later, General Robert Edward Lee officially surrendered in Appomattox, Virginia, in the presence of General Ulysses Simpson Grant.

General Lee and his army surrender to General Grant.

Just as the bloodiest war of the 19th century - with almost 620 000 victims - drew to a close, and the 13th Amendment entrenching the abolition of slavery across the whole of the United States was signed, Lincoln, then at the peak of his glory, was mortally wounded. He was shot in a theatre on 14 April 1865 by John Wilkes Booth, an actor and Confederate sympathiser. Booth was arrested and hanged several days later.

DID YOU KNOW?

The American Civil War gave rise to widespread popular imagery such as the nicknames of Union troops. For example, the name *Yankee* had been used for Northerners since the War of Independence. Attributed to New England inhabitants in the 18th century, the term was used by the British to mean American settlers, particularly those in the North. As such, the term Yankee remained representative of the North to inhabitants of the south.

While the Unionists had no one particular nickname for the southern states, they often referred to them as *Dixies*, a term taken from the Confederate national anthem. Army uniforms also became embedded in popular imagery. The Unionists wore blue, a colour inherited from the American Federal Army, while the Confederates wore grey and brown, being forced to find colours which were easily differentiated from the Union blue.

THE EMANCIPATION PROCLAMATION AND THE 13TH AMENDMENT

Lincoln remained firm in his position towards the Confederates during the whole Civil War. He refused to negotiate with the Confederation, which he considered to be an illegitimate government. As such, victory had to be won on the battlefield. He was also very strict with his generals, reproaching them for their defeats or for not being aggressive enough. He was fond of Ulysses Simpson Grant and his subordinate General Sherman; he admired their tenacity and harsh war practices.

He was somewhat less radical in his approach to prisoners. Since he did not recognise the secession as politically legitimate, he asserted that any prisoners of war were in fact American citizens who could be tried and executed for treason. Lincoln was also uncompromising when it came to African American soldiers captured by rival Confederate troops. The Confederates had announced that any such soldiers would be either executed or sold into slavery, and Lincoln retaliated by declaring that for every African American prisoner killed, a Confederate prisoner would meet the same fate. While the Confederates stopped executing prisoners, their attitude towards slavery remained unchanged.

From the beginning of the Civil War, thousands of slaves fled the South to cross into federal territory or took part in uprisings in Southern plantations. The free African Americans of the North petitioned Lincoln to openly declare support for those mobilising against slave-drivers in the South. A text outlining such support would also put France and Great Britain, who had great political influence, in a delicate position with regards to their own public stance on the situation if they decided to officially recognise the Confederation. From that point on, Lincoln was the Commander in Chief of a country at war, meaning he no longer needed Congress's approval to legislate. Therefore, in September 1862 he announced the emancipation of all slaves in rebel states, effective from 1 January 1863 onwards.

Since this decision was taken in a state of emergency, it still needed to be written into the Constitution to be fully entrenched. This caused heated debate in Congress's two houses, and while the bill was proposed to the Senate and approved in January 1864, it was initially denied approval by the House of Representatives before its eventual approval in January 1865. The ratification from all the states took another year, and it was not until 18 December 1865, eight months after Lincoln's assassination, that the 13th Amendment was officially added to the American Constitution.

CREATING GREENBACKS

During Lincoln's first term as President, American finances had to be used for the Civil War. As such, decisions were taken to find funds for the war which would forever change the country's economic system. Salmon Portland Chase, appointed secretary of the Treasury, found Lincoln to be too moderate in his views and policy. He nonetheless fulfilled his duties very effectively and in 1862, he presented Congress with the Legal Tender Act, a bill which authorised the creation of paper money not backed by gold or silver, to be taken at face value. This led to a new federal banking system being created. Furthermore, the National Banking Acts of 1863 and 1864 unified the monetary system and put an end to the process of each regional bank issuing its own individual currency. In order to nationalise the currency and foster less dependency on private bankers, the Federal Reserve was created.

THE HOMESTEAD ACT AND THE COLONISATION OF THE WEST

In 1862, the Homestead Act was declared. This encouraged westward migration by stipulating that every head of household - called "homesteads" - who had lived on and farmed land for five consecutive years would become its legitimate owner. Furthermore, living on land for six months would reduce the price of purchasing it ($1.25 per acre). During Lincoln's first term, this law allowed 15 000 farmers to purchase their own land. While it was originally aimed at allowing the poorest populations to become landowners, in the end it did little to help them. Before being able to benefit from the new law, families would have to be able to pay for their westward journey, clear their chosen spot of land and build houses and any other construction they needed to survive. As such, many migrants eventually had to sell their newly-acquired plot of land to pay off their debts

This law did however largely contribute to the colonisation of the West, facilitated by new transport policies. It was during the Lincoln administration that the first transcontinental railroad was built. The intention to build was formalised in the *Pacific Railroad Act* of 1862 which launched the first railroad between Omaha, Nebraska and Sacramento, California; almost 3000-kilometres of steel-rimmed tracks.

The construction of the railroad was taken on by two companies - the Central Railroad Company for the Western part of the line and the Union Pacific Railroad for the Eastern part. Work was finished in 1869, when the Eastern and Western tracks were joined together at Promontory Summit, Utah.

IMPACT

THE NORTH-SOUTH ECONOMIC DIVIDE

While the Confederation was unable to repay the debts it had accumulated during the war and the region was plunged into a serious financial crisis, the Union actually found itself in a better financial situation at the end of the war than when it had entered into it. This is largely due to Salmond P. Chase, secretary of the Treasury, and his economic policies.

The North recovered quickly from the Civil War and quickly began to industrialise. Nonetheless, finding capital became difficult and the financial crises which ensued after the war weakened the economy, which was otherwise growing significantly. This growth was facilitated by the construction of new railroads. As this network brought the country closer together, a truly national economy capable of trading with Europe and Asia was able to develop. This new national economy broadened the country's economic perspective, which had previously been constrained by its atomisation to the individual state level.

Reconstructing the economy was a slower and more laborious process in the South. It was after all the battleground of the war; the plantation fields had been ravaged and entire villages destroyed. Furthermore, the plantation economy had been dismantled and the land entrusted to tenant farmers. The loss of the slave workforce should also be noted as a factor contributing to economic transformation. Agriculture rapidly lost ground in the American economy;

in 1839 it accounted for 72% of the economy, by 1899 that figure had dropped to 33%. The southern states would not enjoy a standard of living similar to that of the pre-war years until the middle of the 20th century.

THE END OF SLAVERY

The American social sphere experienced a profound shift due to two phenomena: the end of slavery and European and Asian immigration.

The Civil War sparked an exodus of African American populations from South to North - almost 180 000 African American soldiers had served in the Union armies and 150 00 of them were slaves who came with their families; this figure does not include those who fled persecution. The Lincoln administration and the federal governments which succeeded it were charged with managing an influx of refugees. As such, a system which placed refugees in abandoned farms and plantations, mostly in the Mississippi valley, was put in place.

In the South, there was a true attempt at societal racial integration in the first years after the war. However, this quickly gave way to a system of racial segregation formalised in the Jim Crow laws.

GOOD TO KNOW

Different methods of exclusion were used against African Americans in the South between 1870 and

1880. Policies known as the Jim Crow Laws (named after a popular song which ridiculed African Americans), stipulated strict racial segregation with regards to marriage, burial and daily life. In 1896, the Supreme Court approved these laws in the Plessy v. Ferguson case, ruling that segregation was constitutional so long as separate but equal facilities were provided. It was only in 1954 in the Brown v. Topeka case that segregation was finally declared unconstitutional. All forms of racial discrimination were criminalised in the Civil Rights Act which was passed in 1964.

EUROPEAN AND ASIAN IMMIGRATION

The American West continued to attract migrants throughout Lincoln's presidency, particularly due to the Homestead Act, which allowed farmers to purchase their land after five years of living there, and the development of the Pacific Railroad. These migrants came from diverse backgrounds, searching for the best economic conditions, new lands, new employment prospects and political and religious freedoms. Migrants from Northern Europe largely arrived in the 1850s and were soon after joined by Hispanic populations who had lost their land when Texas, California and New Mexico were created. Chinese migrants took part in the California gold-rush of 1848 and became a huge part of the railroad construction workforce during the Lincoln administration and in the decade which followed.

This migration flow was not restricted to the West. It also gave rise to rapid urbanisation in the East. Originally, immigration was viewed as a positive contribution to the economy, but attitudes towards migrants soon became less favourable. Chinese immigration sparked violence in San Francisco and Los Angeles, leading to the Chinese Exclusion Act in 1882 - the first bill which sought to limit immigration.

The colonisation of the West also revived old tensions with the Native American nations who were essentially exiled to the West in the 1830s as white settlers continued to abusively appropriate their land. The expansion of colonised lands to include the Great Plains posed a severe threat to Native American culture, particularly through endangering bison, the animal at the heart of the culture. Bison became commercial goods in the wake of the boom in trade and commerce. They were increasingly hunted and thus became more and more rare.

POLITICAL REPERCUSSIONS

The ideal of a united American nation was profoundly wounded by the secession and ensuing war; almost a decade was needed to recover some cohesion across all the states. This was brought about through many compromises in both the North and South.

The Civil War reinforced federal executive power. The Lincoln administration had been quick to take decisions without Congress, sometimes almost forcing Congress into certain decisions.

The administration also managed to circumvent the power of the Supreme Court, positioning itself as the highest authority on Constitutional interpretation. Lincoln approached the presidency as a leader, a representative of the people, and considered himself answerable only to them.

After the abolition of slavery was entrenched in the 13th Amendment, two other amendments were announced in 1868 and 1869. The first recognised the citizenship of any person born in the United States and equality among all men. The second banned racial discrimination with regards to citizenship acquisition. There had never been political consensus on emancipated slaves' right to citizenship even in the free states. Lincoln's successor President Andrew Johnson gave only weak support to such a notion and made many explicit or tacit concessions in the South. Thus, the Ku Klux Klan came into being in 1865, led by Southern officers who rejected abolition and any notion of racial equality. They expressed their racist views through violence and terror and were supported both by radical Southern Democrats and by a large section of the population. They launched violent punitive missions and the authorities were forced to intervene. While the federal government dissolved the secret society in 1872 due to escalating violence, it remained silent on the subject of the Jim Crow laws which regularly infringed upon the 14th and 15th Amendments.

SUMMARY

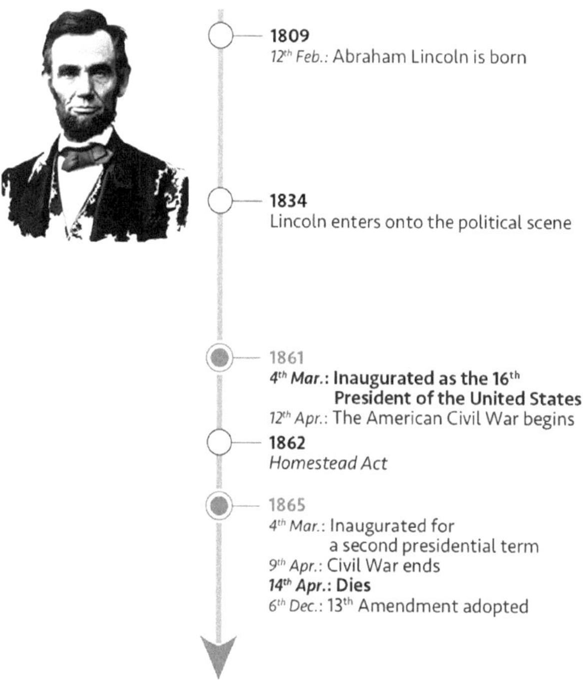

1809
12th Feb.: Abraham Lincoln is born

1834
Lincoln enters onto the political scene

1861
4th Mar.: Inaugurated as the 16th President of the United States
12th Apr.: The American Civil War begins

1862
Homestead Act

1865
4th Mar.: Inaugurated for a second presidential term
9th Apr.: Civil War ends
14th Apr.: Dies
6th Dec.: 13th Amendment adopted

- Abraham Lincoln is born to a modest family on 12 February 1809. He enters the political scene in 1834 and studies law.
- He asserts himself as an abolitionist from the outset, originally from within the Whig Party.
- He is elected to Congress in 1846.
- He is elected as President in November 1860, and sou-

thern states start to secede almost immediately.

- His first presidential term is marked by the Civil War which is responsible for 620 000 deaths and profound economic, political and social change.
- Lincoln announces the Homestead Act in 1862 which encourages the colonisation of western territories. Every "homestead" is entitled to become the owner of a property on which he has lived and worked for a five-year period. The price of land is also reduced after six months of habitation.
- Western colonisation is also facilitated by the development first transcontinental railroad.
- Through several Acts of Congress between 1862 and 1864, Lincoln establishes a new monetary system and a federal banking system which unifies existing financial structures.
- In 1863 and 1865, Lincoln declares the emancipation of all slaves before entrenching the abolition of slavery in the Constitution with the 13th Amendment.
- Lincoln does not live to see the 13th Amendment's final adoption. He is assassinated by a Confederate sympathiser on 14 April 1865.

We want to hear from you!
Leave a comment on your online library
and share your favourite books on social media!

FIND OUT MORE

BIBLIOGRAPHY

- Ameur, F. (2004) *La guerre de Sécession*. Paris: PUF.
- Bruce, D.K. (1954) *Les présidents des USA de George Washington à Abraham Lincoln*. Paris: Gallimard.
- Desbiens, A. (2012) *Histoire des États-Unis. Des origines à nos jours*. Paris: Éditions du Nouveau Monde.
- Duncan, A. (2007) La guerre de Sécession. *Revue d'histoire du xixe siècle*. 1(35), pp. 141-159.
- Faulkner, H.U. (1958) *Une histoire économique des États-Unis d'Amérique, des origines à nos jours*. Paris: PUF.
- Fohlen, C. (2007) *Histoire de l'esclavage aux États-Unis*. Paris: Perrin.
- Jonas, R. A. (1997) Le prix de la paix. Un regard vendéen sur la guerre de Sécession. *Annales de Bretagne et des pays de l'Ouest*. 104(1), pp. 89-98.
- Kaspi, A. (1992) *La guerre de Sécession. Les États désunis*. Paris: Gallimard.
- McPherson, J. M. (1991) *La guerre de Sécession (181-1865)*. Paris: Robert Laffont.
- Mélandri, P. (2008) *Histoire des États-Unis contemporains*. Brussels: André Versailles.
- Oates, S. B. (1984) *Lincoln*. Paris: Fayard.
- Portes, J. (2010) *Histoire des États-Unis. De 1776 à nos jours*. Paris: Armand Colin.

ICONOGRAPHIC SOURCES

- Portrait of Abraham Lincoln, dated 1863. Royalty-free reproduction picture.
- The bombing of Fort Sumter. Royalty-free reproduction picture.
- The assassination of President Lincoln. Royalty-free reproduction picture.
- General Lee and his army surrender to General Grant. Royalty-free reproduction picture.

FILMS

- *Lincoln.* (2012) [Film]. Steven Spielberg. Dir. USA: Dreamworks SKG.

IMPROVE YOUR GENERAL KNOWLEDGE

IN A BLINK OF AN EYE !

www.50minutes.com

www.50minutes.com

ISBN ebook: 9782806276117

ISBN paper: 9782806282927

Legal Deposit: D/2016/12603/291

Cover: © Primento

Digital conception by Primento, the digital partner of publishers.